SUBMARINES
US Navy Submariners
100-Page Activity and Coloring Book

This Book Belongs To:

____

My Submarine Veteran is: ________________________________

They served in the Navy - From ____________ **To** __________

He/She served in the Navy on the following submarines:

1. ____
2. ____
3. ____
4. ____

He/She Earned their Dolphins on: ___________________

His/Her Rate/Rank is/was ________________________________

TheEnchantedTreehouse.com

Visit Website for
FREE Coloring Pages

My _________________________________ served
in the United States Navy.

SUBMARINES

Submarines are ships that travel underneath the ocean.

SAILORS

There are over 100 sailors on a submarine
crew when they go to sea.

FAST-ATTACK

Some submarine sailors served on fast-attack submarines.

BOOMER

Some submarine sailors served on missile boats or 'Boomers'.

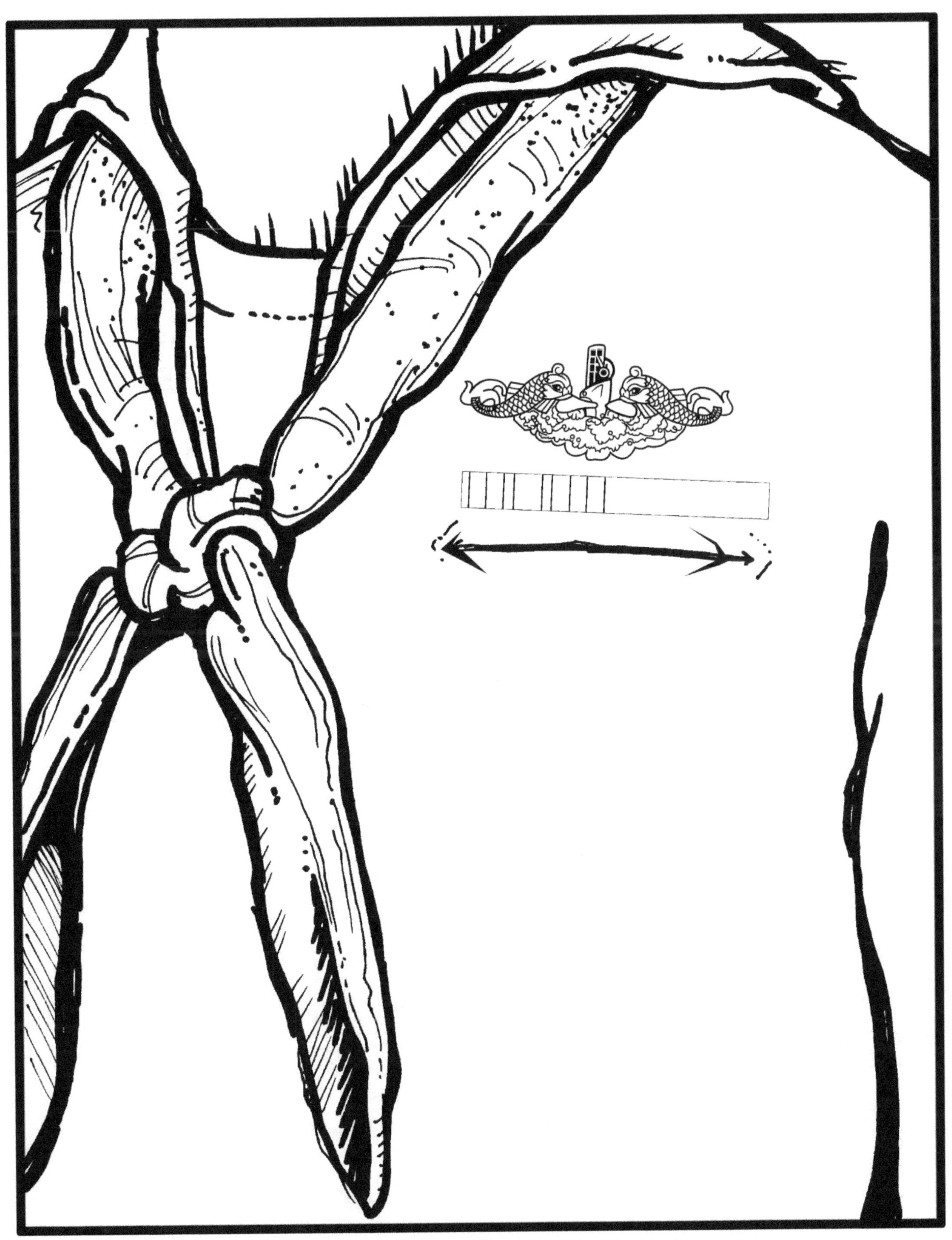

**All submarine sailors have to earn their Dolphins.
They wear their Dolphins on their uniforms over their hearts.**

PATROLS

Submarines go to sea for long periods of time called patrols. Sometimes patrols last for many months at a time.

**Boomer submarine sailors also wear a patrol pen.
Each star represents a deterrent patrol they made.**

USN SUBMARINE FORCE

RUN SILENT, RUN DEEP!

The Silent Service

Submarines have to be very quiet when they go
to sea to stay hidden from other subs and ships.

SONAR

Submarines can listen underwater using SONAR.

They can hear other ships on the surface and other submarines if they are not quiet.

BIOLOGICS

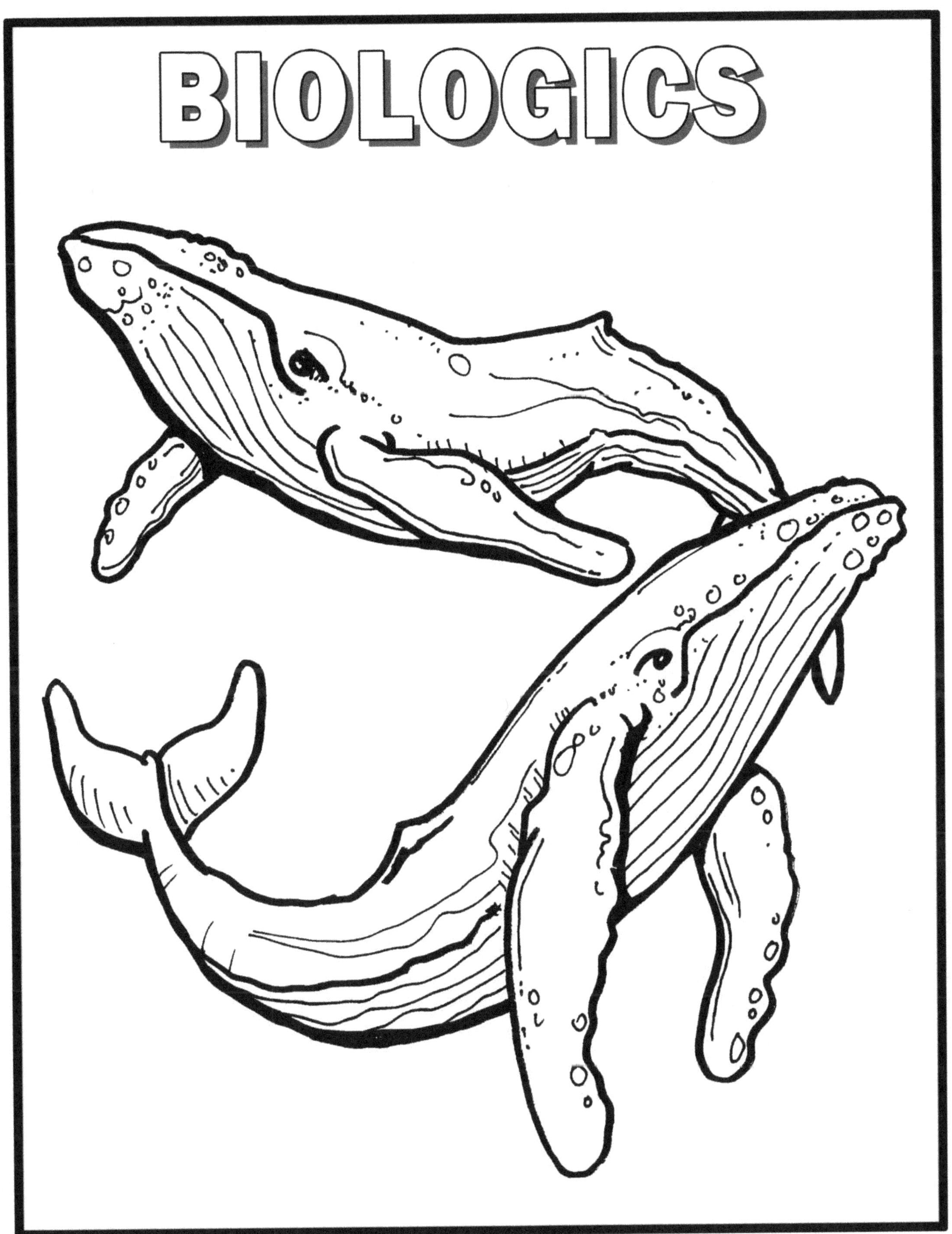

Sometimes they can hear whales and other animals
under the water that are singing or making noises.

Most all submarines can shoot torpedoes. Only Boomers can shoot missiles and they launch them from underwater.

TRIDENT

The largest US Boomers are call Tridents
and they carry 24 missiles onboard.

The newest class of US submarines are the
Virginia Class or Seawolf Submarines.

BROACH

Sometime submarines test their emergency blow systems that cause the sub to 'broach' or pop up out of the water.

Nuclear submarines have a power plant onboard that produces electricity to power all the equipment onboard...

... including the motors to turn the 'Screw' that pushes the boat through the water .

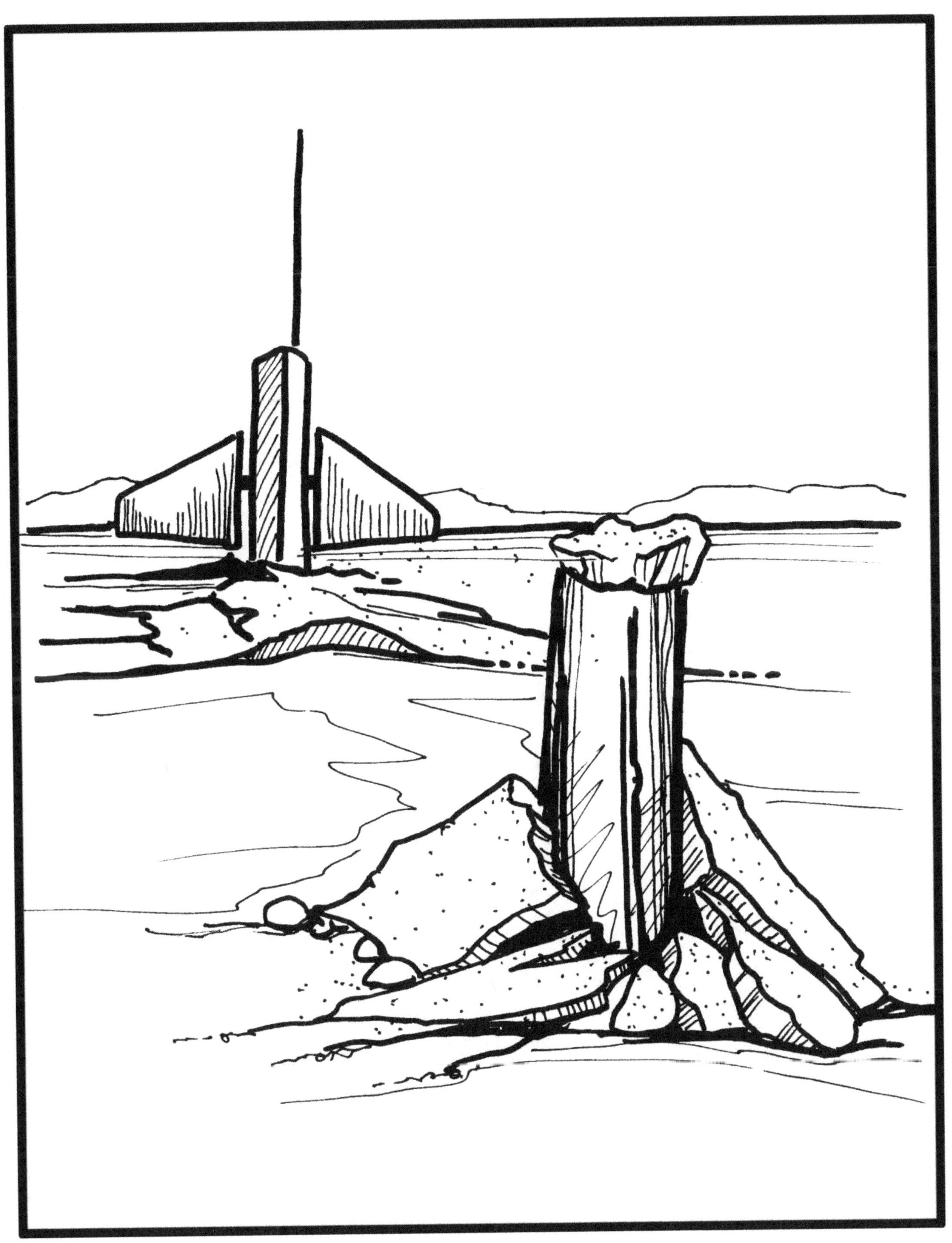

Some submarines are designed to break
through the ice near the North Pole.

Did You Know? Fun Fact

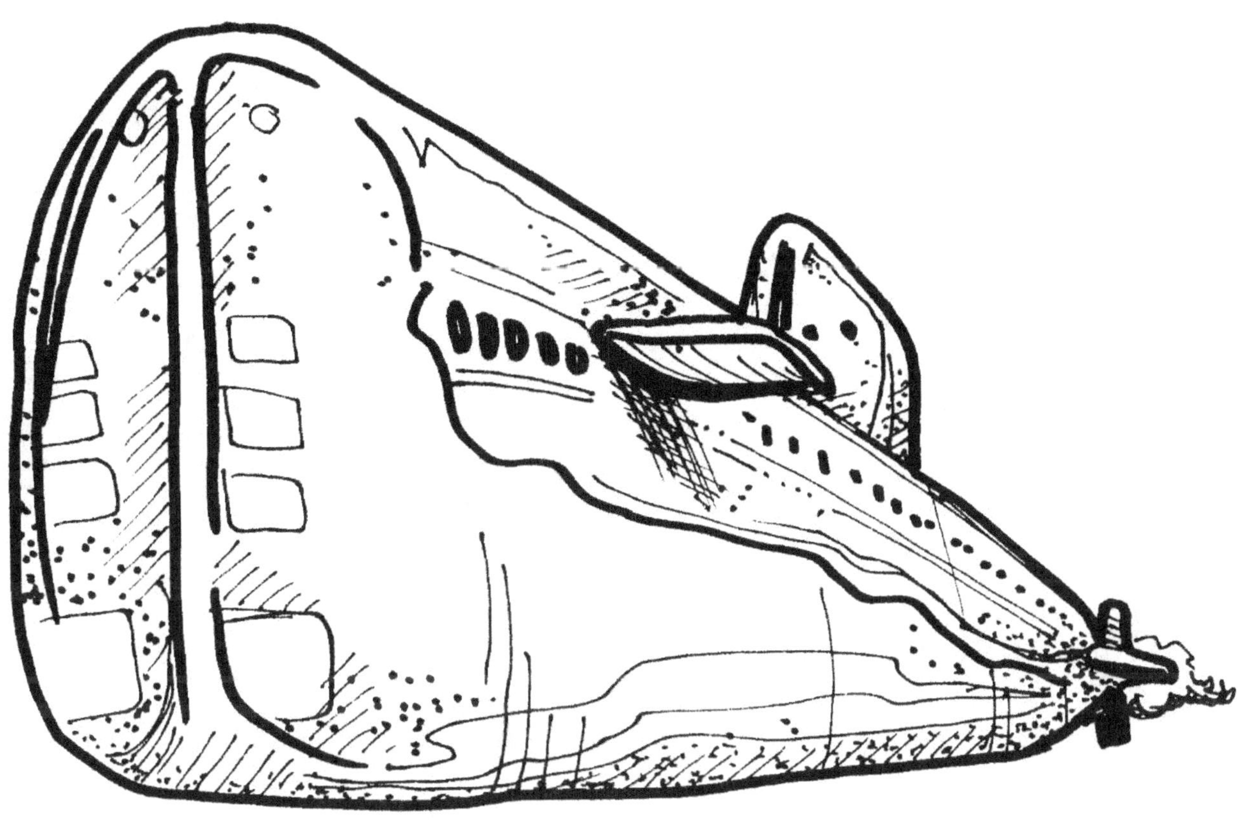

The Nautilus was launched in 1954 and was the first nuclear submarine. It was able to go faster and stay underwater longer than other diesel-electric submarines that were also being used.

The first nuclear-powered submarine was the USS Nautilus.

Some submarines are designed to break
through the ice near the North Pole.

1 ACROSS - A long period at sea.

1 DOWN - A submerged submarine's looking device.

2 DOWN - A type of power plant on Navy submarines.

3 ACROSS - A ship that can travel underwater.

4 ACROSS - The award earned by qualified submariners.

Crossword Puzzle

H D O L P H I N S N S H
E W R F F R U L P J D
W T G G D T B J D K
F F Y N U C L E A R
N P I N N G A J J Y R
U N D E R W A T E R R
D M I S S I L E D S
P E R I S C O P E U
Q T O R P E D O P B
I V N R K V U R A M
S J A H S P V K T A
T R M W O Y E Q R R
E J Z M N N K M O I N
D B T A A R R Q L N
W C R D R A R Z I E

Periscope **Patrol** **Torpedo**
Dolphins **Nuclear** **Underwater**
Submarine **Missile** **Sonar**

Word Search Puzzle

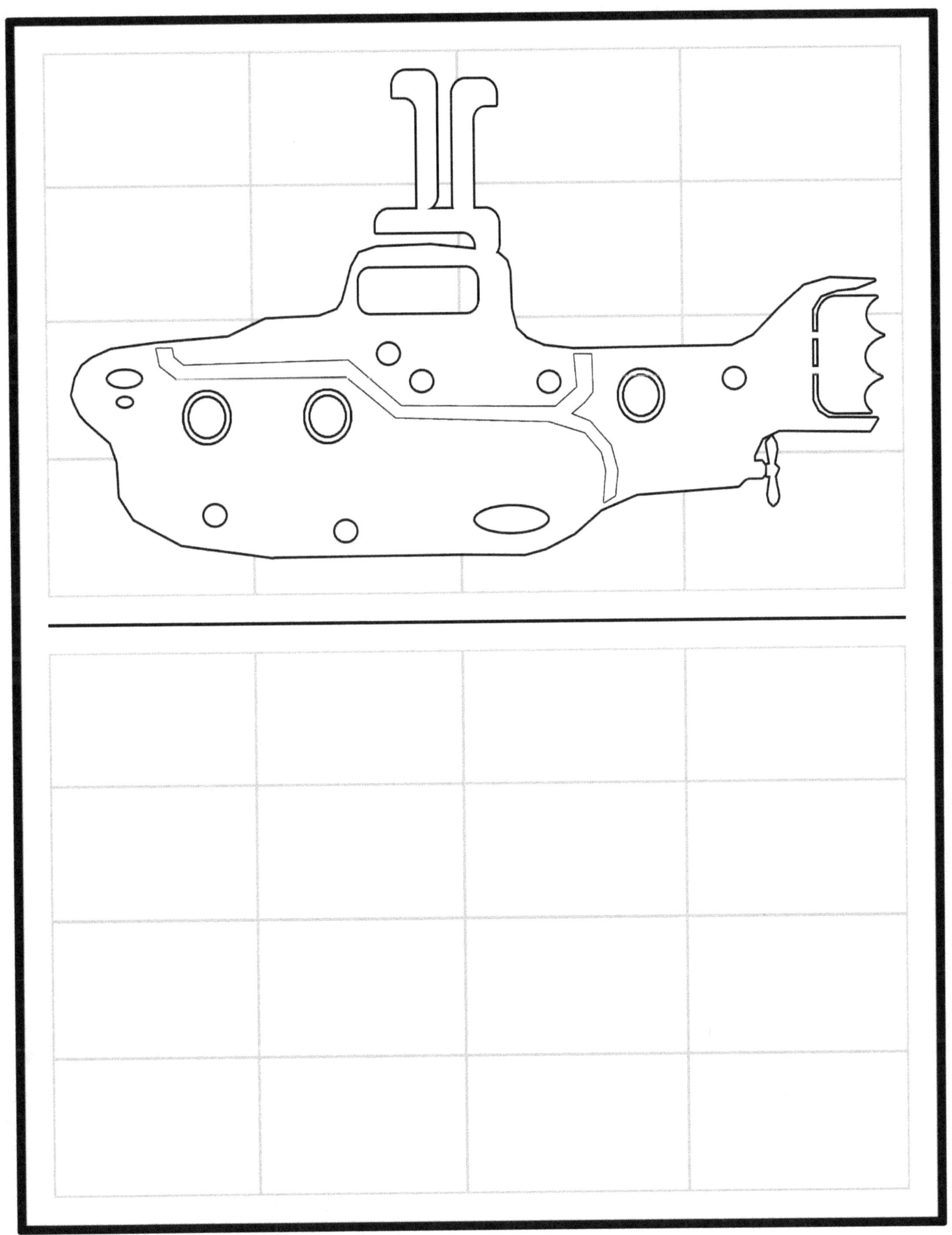

Can you draw the submarine?

Submarine MISSILE Comparison

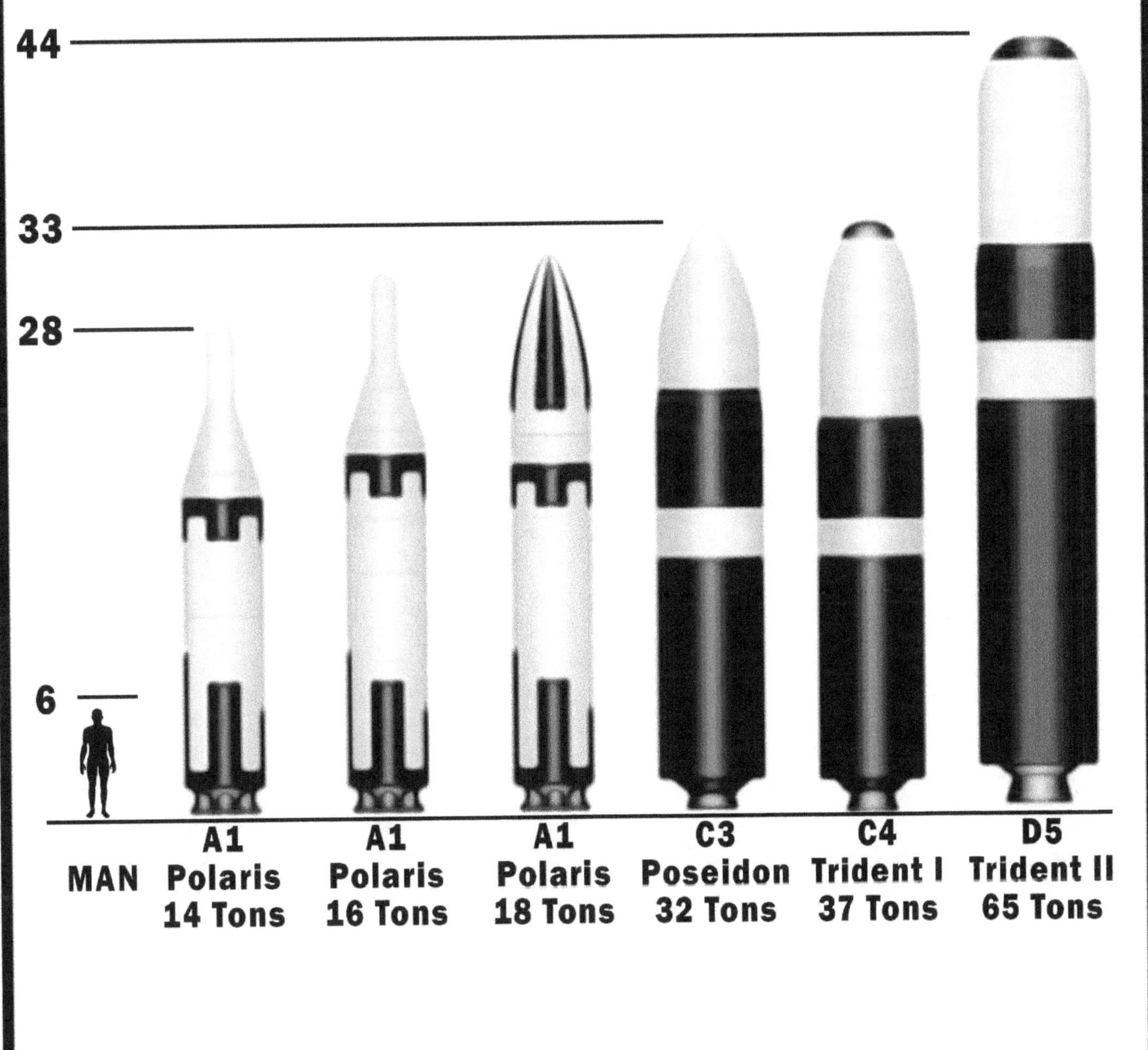

Missile Comparison

HAPPY BIRTHDAY

The United States Navy traces its origins to the Continental Navy, which was established at the beginning of the American Revolution.

Submarine Birthday - April 11, 1900

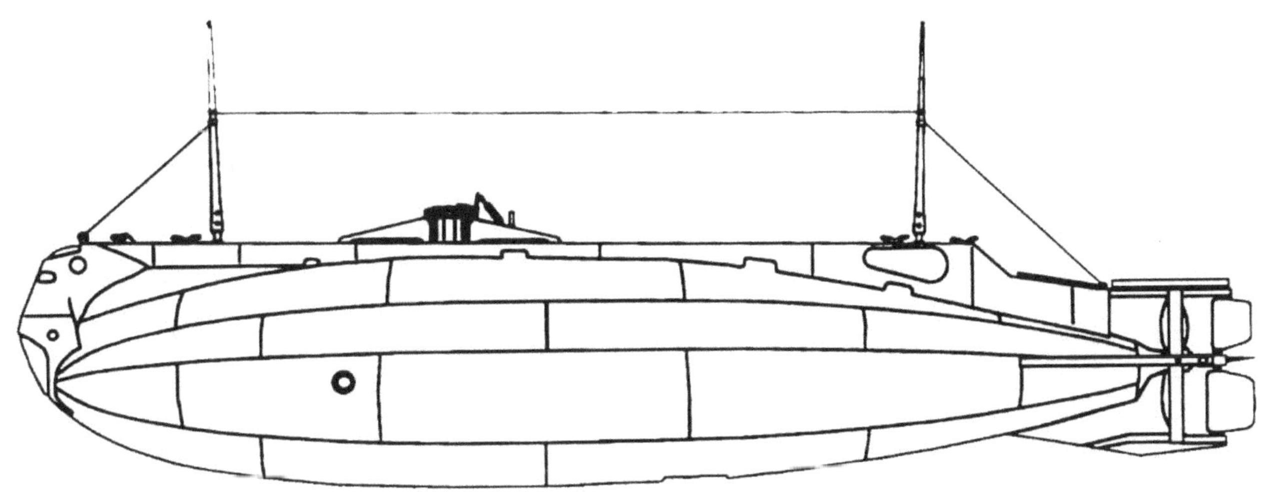

On April 11, 1900, the United States Navy acquired its first commissioned submarine, the USS Holland.

Submarine Maze

HAPPY BIRTHDAY

The United States Navy traces its origins to the Continental Navy, which was established at the beginning of the American Revolution.

Submarine Birthday - April 11, 1900

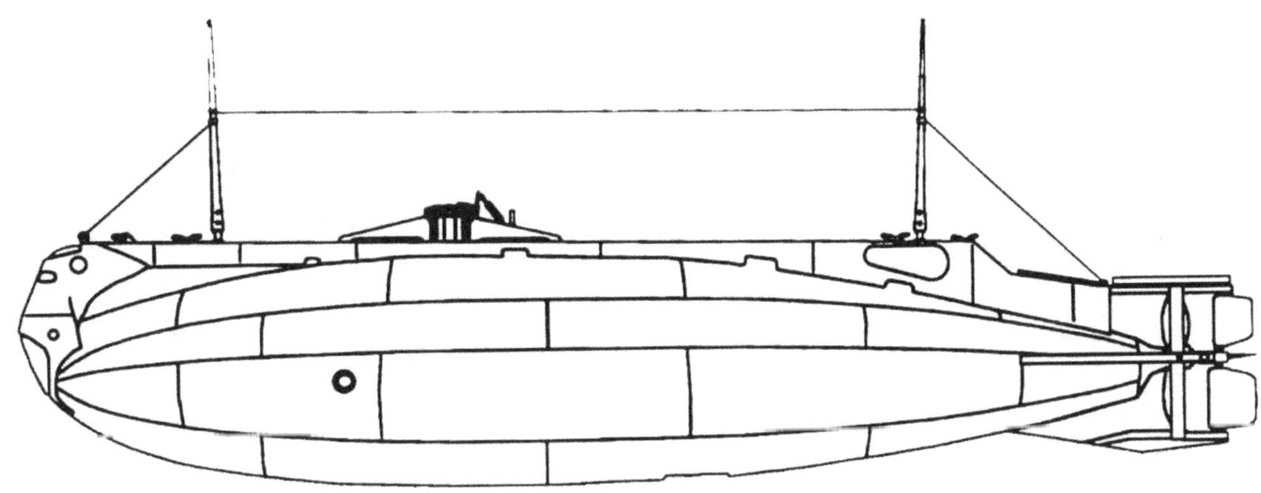

On April 11, 1900, the United States Navy acquired its first commissioned submarine, the USS Holland.

STS/SS Tim Thomas, 1984 - 1989

Dedicated to the crews of the USS Stonewall Jackson SSBN 634
and all US Submarine Sailors in the US Navy.

The End